FAO Ethics Series No. 1
Ethical issues in food and agriculture

CORRIGENDUM

Page 14, Figure 1
The legend for the right-hand scale (Atlantic cod catch)
and the related curve on the graph (Total cod catch)
should read "Atlantic cod catch for North America".

TC/M/X9601E
ISBN 92-5-104559-3
ISSN 0081-4539

1

Ethical issues in
food and agriculture

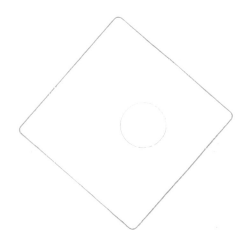

Plea
show

Ren

Textpl
speec

www.
L32

FOOD AND AGRICULTURE ORGANIZATION OF THE UNITED NATIONS
Rome, 2001

Editing, design, graphics and desktop publishing:
Editorial Group
FAO Information Division

The designations employed and the presentation of material in this information product do not imply the expression of any opinion whatsoever on the part of the Food and Agriculture Organization of the United Nations concerning the legal status of any country, territory, city or area or of its authorities, or concerning the delimitation of its frontiers or boundaries.

ISBN 92-5-104559-3

Foreword

The stubborn persistence of hunger and poverty raises what are perhaps the most burning ethical questions of our age. Freeing humanity from hunger and malnutrition is a moral obligation that weighs on us more and more heavily as our capabilities and technologies advance. The world undoubtedly has the productive capacity to produce adequate quantities of nutritious food for all, yet gross inequities in people's access to resources, opportunities and – not least – fair representation perpetuate the hunger and deprivation of more than 800 million people today.

Technological advances and organizational changes affecting food and agriculture systems over the past years have been both radical and rapid; their repercussions, however, will be felt for a long time to come and, in many cases, the consequences may be irreversible. Whether they be as specific as individual food production techniques, or as broad as the effects of globalized international trade, such changes have refocused attention on fundamental human rights, including the right to sufficient – and safe – food. Science continues to broaden our horizons, offering us new options that invariably give rise to controversy. Not surprisingly, recent developments have brought to the fore numerous ethical issues that are central to food security and to sustainable rural development and natural resource management; they are therefore of prime concern to FAO.

FAO has an obligation to ensure that its actions are responsible, transparent and accountable, thus ethical considerations are inherent in the Organization's programmes. In respect of the human right to democratic participation, for example, in all of its activities FAO seeks to foster equity and the free and meaningful involvement of all stakeholders. It advocates the sustainable management of natural resources and – with regard to food production and processing technologies in particular – the containment of risks to human health, today and in the future. The Organization's very mission – helping to build a food-secure world for present and future generations – implies the promotion of sustainability, which is itself of major ethical significance.

It is also FAO's duty to facilitate debate and dialogue concerning ethics and human rights in fields related to its sphere of work – examples of salient areas being genetic resources, biotechnology applications and biosecurity issues. With the aim of stimulating international discussion and deepening the general understanding of key ethical issues, we are now launching a specific publications series to treat this multifaceted subject. The present publication, the first in the series, introduces ethical questions as they relate to FAO's mandate and describes a vision for building an ethical and equitable food and agriculture framework. Based on respect for the diversity of human value systems and designed to enhance public health and well-being as well as environmental conservation, such a framework should be an ongoing participatory process; it should evolve over time in response to fresh knowledge, changes in objectives and new ethical issues raised by FAO and its partners – including consumers and producers.

The importance attached to the ethical dimension of FAO's programmes is manifest in the formal designation of ethics as a priority area for interdisciplinary action across the Organization. To provide guidance and determine the scope of ethical issues relevant to our mandate, I have set up an internal FAO Committee on Ethics in Food and Agriculture. In addition, I have established an entirely independent Panel of Eminent Experts, both to advise the Organization and raise public awareness and understanding. It is my hope, furthermore, that ethical concerns will be integrated into debates within FAO's governing bodies as well as in other intergovernmental fora. I believe these initiatives are crucial to furthering the integration of ethical considerations in decisions regarding global food security and poverty alleviation. •

Jacques Diouf
FAO Director-General

Contents

For the first time, the development of the food and agriculture sector is being conceptualized globally – as indeed it must be

Introduction

In recent years food and agriculture have undergone major changes, including rapid technological advances, a restructuring of the resource base, the creation of new and expanded international markets, and closer ties with environmental management. For the first time, the development of the food and agriculture sector is being conceptualized globally – as indeed it must be. A fiscal crisis in Asia may depress farm prices in North America. A crop failure in Latin America may raise prices in Africa, while an exceptionally bountiful harvest may have the reverse effect, leaving surpluses in granaries unsold. Environmental pollution in one nation may reduce timber yields in another. A food-borne disease originating in one farmer's field may wreak havoc in several continents.

As a result of these developments, all societies have some point of convergence with one another. A tractor built in North America can be used to cultivate a field in Central Asia. A poultry processing plant in Brazil will be much the same as one in Thailand. Conformity to Codex Alimentarius standards is becoming *de facto* mandatory as a result of the formation of the World Trade Organization. In virtually every large city on earth, it is possible to buy pizza made with similar ingredients, eat at a "fast food" restaurant and drink the same bottled soft drinks. Shipping containers, pallets, food packages and air cargo planes are all tending towards uniformity as world trade increases.

Yet the new technologies, institutions, business practices, marketing systems and intellectual property rights that are available globally cannot be considered neutral in cultural terms. They challenge age-old and deeply held values and, in particular, the new technologies and institutions often carry with them hidden assumptions. These include specific (usually Western) definitions of private property rights, a bias against common property resources, an emphasis on individual initiative rather than respect for family or community traditions, greater attention to formal contracts, protection against the worst excesses of monopolies and even a knowledge of English.

In Western nations, where technological change and market-oriented operations are widely accepted, value differences have emerged for a range of issues, including animal welfare, genetically modified foods, use of designations of origins, and acceptable levels of economic concentration in the food and agriculture system. In some other nations, "free" markets are a recent advent. In nations where the charging of interest is considered illegitimate or the person or entity with whom one trades is more important than the price, the new global economy has met with considerable resistance. Moreover, throughout the world, fair representation and the expression of public opinion are thwarted: the least developed nations have neither the funds nor the expertise to participate meaningfully in global debates and, even in Western nations, a significant portion of the population remains disenfranchised, as evidenced by the recent demonstrations in Seattle and Geneva.

Insofar as all these changes bring with them the potential for conflict and social upheaval, they have brought to the fore numerous ethical issues that are central to food security, sustainable rural development and resource management as well as to the trade-offs among these objectives. The resolution of issues raised demands reflection, dialogue and action.

This paper[1] addresses ethical questions as they relate to FAO's mandate. First, the values central to food and agriculture are identified. Following this, the current situation is examined and specific issues are analysed. It is then argued that the balancing of interests and the peaceful resolution of conflicts should be common global goals. The last section describes a vision for building an ethical, efficient and safe world food and agriculture framework that is equitable and solidary and that respects the diversity of value systems. •

---

[1] A draft version of this paper was made available to the Panel of Eminent Experts on Ethics on Food and Agriculture during its first session in September 2000.

Ethics in food and agriculture

The production, transformation and distribution of food and agricultural products are generally accepted as routine aspects of daily life around the world. Therefore, such activities have rarely been addressed within the realm of ethics. But food and agriculture, and the economic benefits that derive from participation in the food and agriculture system, are means to ends that are inherently ethical in nature. Only on a few occasions has FAO considered ethical values, although they are embedded in the preamble to the Organization's Constitution (see Box). Without these ethical values, the most important of which are considered below, FAO would have little reason to exist.

The value of food. Food is essential for the survival of human beings; hunger results from neglect of the universal right to food. Both formal ethical systems and ethical practices in every society presume the necessity of providing those who are able-bodied with the means to obtain food and enabling those who are unable to feed themselves to receive food directly. Failure to do so is deemed an injustice, an unethical act, whereas the elimination of hunger and malnutrition is deemed beneficent. Several international documents proclaim the validity of this well-established principle, among them the Universal Declaration of Human Rights (1948) and the Rome Declaration on World Food Security (1996).

The value of enhanced well-being. Today, nearly every nation state recognizes the need to enhance the well-being of its citizens. Such improvements in well-being also advance human dignity and self-respect. While charity is sometimes necessary to respond to desperate and pressing situations, it cannot provide for long-term improvements in well-being, which can only be accomplished by providing people with access to skills, capital, employment, education and opportunities. In addition, for sustainable agriculture and rural development to flourish, a viable rural infrastructure must be in place, together with an enabling policy environment.

The value of human health. Human health is improved by the elimination of hunger and malnutrition. Healthy people are more able to participate in human affairs and more able to live productive and meaningful lives. Furthermore, the protection of human health also involves ensuring adequate nutrition and safeguards against unsafe food. On both of these points, nations are agreed – as members of the World Health Organization (WHO Constitution, 1946) and the Codex Alimentarius Commission (1963).

Excerpt from the Preamble to FAO's Constitution

The Nations accepting this Constitution, being determined to promote the common welfare by furthering separate and collective action on their part for the purpose of:

- raising levels of nutrition and standards of living of the peoples under their respective jurisdictions;
- securing improvements in the efficiency of the production and distribution of all food and agricultural products;
- bettering the condition of rural populations;
- and thus contributing towards an expanding world economy and ensuring humanity's freedom from hunger;

hereby establish the Food and Agriculture Organization of the United Nations ...

The value of natural resources. All human societies recognize the importance of natural resources, which are those parts of the natural world that are used to produce food and other valued goods and which are necessary for our survival and prosperity. Clearly, no particular use of such resources should undermine the other legitimate uses to which they might be put, now or in the future. In particular, no current use should condemn our progeny to endless toil or deprivation.

The value of nature. Finally, there is growing agreement that nature itself must be valued. As our power to modify nature grows, there is also an increasing recognition of the beauty, complexity and integrity of nature, and of the limits to humans' restructuring of the natural world. The Convention on Biological Diversity (1992) not only recognizes the value that may be placed on particular organisms; it also acknowledges, as do countless cultures, that nature itself is to be valued for what it is.

* * *

To sum up, these values define in part who we are and what we should do and, while different cultures may vary in their interpretation of them, all agree as to their importance. The values in question are by no means new, and they are also central to FAO's mission. So why is it that they are again the subject of dialogue and debate? Why is it that FAO feels obliged to raise the issue of ethics in food and agriculture? •

Current trends

Today, ethical concerns are central to debates about the kind of future people want. This is the result of several profound changes that are affecting virtually everyone on the planet and forcing people to come to grips with the limits of particular cultural perspectives. These changes, or trends, are considered below.

Human population growth and demographic shifts

The global population is increasing to unprecedented levels, posing challenges to food production and distribution. Although fertility rates are declining almost everywhere, global population growth will continue well into the twenty-first century (Figure 1). The world's population is currently projected to reach approximately 9 billion by 2050. As a result of low birth rates, combined with improvements in life expectancy, many developed countries have recorded rapid increases in the proportion of elderly people as a population group and, in some cases, even a decline in their overall population.

FIGURE 1
Projected population growth

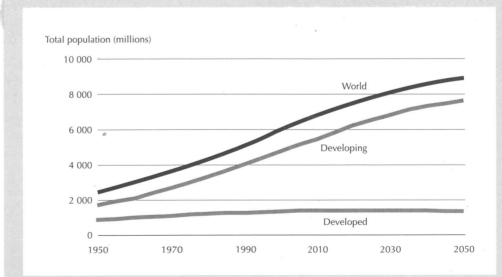

Source: FAOSTAT, 2000.

In contrast, developing countries generally have much younger population structures. Rural-to-urban migration continues in many parts of the globe, leading to a world that will soon have more urban than rural inhabitants. Given that young adults account for the majority of migratory moves, rural-urban migration tends to accelerate demographic ageing in rural areas, resulting in considerable shrinkages in the rural labour force. This will have profound consequences for agriculture, as the transportation and processing of food products and people's ability to purchase them become even more essential as components of food security.

Human populations and their food supplies can both be affected by disease. Although major strides were made in controlling disease during the last century, new and resurgent diseases are a source of suffering and decreased productivity. For example, new antibiotic-resistant tuberculosis strains and dangerous *Escherichia coli* strains are a threat to human populations worldwide. AIDS is found mostly among people who are of working age, cutting sharply into the agricultural and industrial workforce. At the same time, in tropical nations malaria and other diseases continue to take their toll through illness and death. Food-borne disease is a common cause of morbidity and mortality everywhere. Illness alone is not likely to affect the total food supply but, in an increasingly urban world, it can be expected to reduce many people's access to food.

Pressure on natural resources

In many areas of the world, plant and animal genetic resources, land, air, water, forests and wetlands – the renewable natural resources upon which human life is dependent – are being rapidly degraded. In some nations, this is the result of the desperation of poverty; in wealthy nations, it is a consequence of disincentives for producers and consumers to ensure conservation practices.

Ancient systems for the maintenance of common property resources, including fisheries and forestry, genetic resources and rangelands, are under increasing pressure from both population growth and increasing market penetration. In the search for more farmland, huge areas are being deforested, leading to soil erosion and massive flooding.

The renewable natural resources upon which human life is dependent are being rapidly degraded in many areas of the world

Overuse of marginal lands continues apace, turning fields into deserts and depriving future generations of vital crop and pasture land. Simultaneously, misuse of irrigation water is depleting aquifers and causing the salinization of fertile lands.

FAO/18829/I. BALDERI

Industrialization of agriculture

Improvements in communications and transportation have now brought most producers and consumers into a global market

GRAMEENPHONE LTD

Once largely the province of smallholders, today agriculture is an increasingly large-scale business in many parts of the world. Farmers are more and more dependent on input suppliers for seeds, fertilizers, machinery and pesticides. At the same time, they must often be responsive to large food retailers who demand particular agronomic practices and set delivery dates and quality characteristics. Smallholders and farmworkers, particularly women, are often among those to be forced out of activity or bypassed by these transformations. Industrial inputs are often subsidized, replacing farmworkers with machines or exposing them to toxic chemicals. A disproportionately large number of women are displaced and often have great difficulty in obtaining alternative employment.

While increased supplies and declining prices of farm products result in less expensive food for the urban poor, they also cause the displacement of smallholders or reduce them to bare subsistence. Industrialization also brings greater risks, as crop plants and domestic animals become more genetically uniform. Whereas in the past, myriads of smallholders maintained the biodiversity necessary for the continued viability of crops and domestic animals, today national governments and international treaties are increasingly requested to manage the earth's biodiversity.

Concentration of economic power

While global production is reaching increasingly high levels, economic power is becoming more concentrated. The net worth of the world's 200 richest people is greater than the combined income of 41 percent of the world's population. The world's 200 largest transnational corporations now account for a quarter of the world's economic activity. In the food and agriculture sector, mergers and acquisitions are rapidly reducing to single digits the number of companies engaged in input production, food processing and food retailing. In some nations, landownership is also becoming increasingly concentrated. This has occurred simultaneously with the withdrawal of nation states from various activities of the food and agriculture sector. For example, the agenda for agricultural research and extension, once the domain of the state, is now largely set in the private sector.

Thus, much of the research on crops and livestock that does not hold the potential to generate private profit has been abandoned as the presence of the state has diminished. As a result, marginal stakeholder groups, including smallholders, farmworkers and poor consumers, are in danger of losing what little voice they had in research policy decisions.

Globalization

Although long-distance trade was known to the ancient world, improvements in communications and transportation as well as the liberalization of trade have now brought most producers and consumers into a global market. The interdependencies created in this manner have the potential to generate greater global solidarity. Yet the rules for this new global economy are only partially written and are themselves the subject of considerable contention.

Global competition may result in lower prices, but it also erodes cultural values and national identities. It may also foreclose options for future generations. Moreover, while textbook accounts suggest that trade liberalization will lead to greater overall welfare, some actors have the wherewithal to take advantage of global markets to a far greater extent than others, owing to their access to capital, expertise, technologies and policy-makers. Conversely, others benefit much less and even suffer losses, often through no fault of their own. Furthermore, only in a few situations are people who are unfairly denied access to these means compensated or provided with alternative opportunities to help themselves.

Human-induced change

Today many, if not most, of the emergencies (famine, crop failure, floods, drought and war) faced by nations and regions are at least partially the result of human-induced change (Figure 2). Humans' ability to modify the global landscape, together with an increasing population, enable them to engage in actions that transform societies and the natural world in unintended and/or unforeseeable ways. The most obvious consequence is what is now defined as global climate change – the raising of the earth's temperature as a result of greenhouse gas emissions, generated by the burning of fossil fuels in power generation, industry and transport. Less apparent are the ways in which human activities, such as deforestation, building on floodplains, depletion of groundwater supplies and even responses to disasters themselves, may contribute to "natural" disasters. Often, those who bear the brunt

Human-induced environmental changes may contribute to "natural" disasters

FAO/20669/E. YEVES

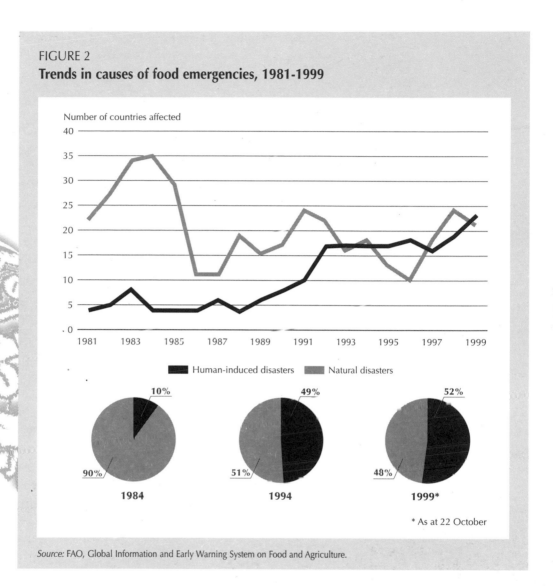

FIGURE 2

Trends in causes of food emergencies, 1981-1999

Number of countries affected

Human-induced disasters ■   Natural disasters ■

10%
90%
1984

49%
51%
1994

52%
48%
1999*

* As at 22 October

Source: FAO, Global Information and Early Warning System on Food and Agriculture.

of these emergencies are the nations with small developing economies, the rural poor, women and children. These groups are also the least able to become self-reliant without external aid.

New biotechnologies

For millennia, the food and agriculture system has made use of biotechnologies in the form of fermented foods such as bread, cheese and beer. But the new biotechnologies, at once a collection of tools for research and new means of generating food and agricultural products, hold even greater promise – and some risk. Biotechnol-

Certain biotechnologies have been used to generate food and agricultural products for millenia; the new technologies are expanding that capacity even further

ogies could help to increase the supply, diversity and quality of food products, reduce costs of production and processing and reduce pesticide use and environmental degradation. They could also be used to develop new animal vaccines, improve food safety, prolong storage and change the nutritional content of foods.

Biotechnology includes a wide range of different techniques, many of which are not controversial, as well as the process referred to as genetic engineering. Central to this process is the ability to select and manipulate genetic material with great precision and to transfer traits of interest from one species to express them in another. Biotechnology also encompasses the creation of cloned organisms, such as Dolly (the renowned cloned sheep), and the modification of reproductive mechanisms. However, the ability to transfer genes in no way infers knowledge of which genes should be transferred.

Given the trend of state withdrawal from agricultural research, most successful applications developed with genetic engineering to date have been those that are profitable for their predominantly private sector developers. This is true of herbicide tolerance and insect resistance, for example. Combined with restrictive intellectual property laws, such applications may become means for further concentrating economic power. In addition, although there is little empirical evidence as yet, these products may pose new risks, both for the environment and human health. Examples include the transfer of herbicide tolerance to weeds, leading to more aggressive or more competitive weeds; the transfer of food allergenic compounds to products that did not previously contain them; and the replacement of diverse native populations with more uniform and aggressive genetically engineered varieties. An extreme scenario could be the use of the new biotechnologies for bioterrorism.

Informatics

Information technology today is transforming the speed as well as the ways in which people communicate with one another in much the same way as the telephone and telegraph did a century ago. In principle, with a small amount of equipment, anyone can communicate with another person on the planet at any time. In the food and agriculture sector, modern information and communication technologies have enormous potential for wide and rapid knowledge sharing at all stages of the food chain. For example, it allows precision farming – farming guided by detailed environmental information so as to minimize the use of water, agrochemicals and labour. When combined with emerging nanotechnologies (which permit manipulation and manufacture at the molecular level), informatics may permit vast increases in production efficiencies as well.

However, access to the new information technologies is highly unequal. Even in the industrialized nations, the poor lack access to the new media. In much of the developing world, only a few have access to telephones, and only a minute élite can afford the new technologies. In addition, just as informatics can speed up constructive political, commercial and familial communication, it can also facilitate communication for destructive purposes. Generally, these new technologies can intrude on the private lives of citizens in ways that were never possible before.

* * *

Each of the points briefly discussed above raises profound ethical questions that FAO must address in carrying out its mandated activities. The points covered are inextricably connected. Urbanization and industrialized agriculture have massively enhanced world trade, increased the world's total material wealth and prosperity, greatly expanded the scope of people's diets, reduced the cost and increased the abundance of basic cereals, and shifted value in the food and agriculture system from the farm to the input and post-harvest sectors. At the same time, however, these transformations have posed new problems – problems that are at once material and ethical. ●

The issues

Bias against the poor

Perhaps the most egregious problem is the widespread bias against the hungry and the poor. Most societies were once structured so that, even though many people were poor, most had access to sufficient food to ensure their survival. Social,

FAO/17030/G. BIZZARRI

Social, economic and technological changes have left the poor with limited access to land and water – women in rural areas are often the worst affected

economic and technological changes have since eroded the traditional "safety nets", and ties to the land have been weakened or severed, making it difficult or impossible for the poor to grow their own food. In quite a few rural areas today, archaic and inequitable agrarian structures have been grafted on to highly industrialized agricultural production systems, leaving the poor with limited access to land, water, fuelwood and other basic amenities (Figure 3). Poor women in rural areas, in particular, are often forced to spend much of their time searching for water and fuelwood with which to prepare meagre meals for their families.

Once primarily the result of crop failure in isolated areas, famine today is increasingly caused by the marginalization and impoverishment of rural populations as a result of inadequate institutions and policies. Marginalization and impoverishment have multiple causes but they often result from a lack of viable resource alternatives, with a consequent reliance on marginal lands and deforestation. Chronic undernutrition and malnutrition, indicators of serious vulnerability to natural or human-induced emergencies, are often observed in such populations. Civil strife and war are also fuelled by such processes and further weaken food security. These conditions often lead to vast population movements, especially from rural to urban areas and often across national borders.

In urban areas, furthermore, crowding, inadequate sanitation, makeshift housing, longer food transport networks and a lack of clean water often lead to the rapid spread of disease and malnutrition, sapping poor people's ability to care for themselves and undermining the mental development of their children. All this is exac-

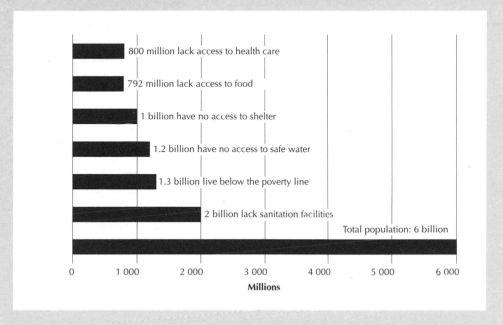

FIGURE 3
Number of people living in poverty or lacking access to essential services in the developing world

800 million lack access to health care

792 million lack access to food

1 billion have no access to shelter

1.2 billion have no access to safe water

1.3 billion live below the poverty line

2 billion lack sanitation facilities

Total population: 6 billion

0   1 000   2 000   3 000   4 000   5 000   6 000

Millions

Source. FAO. 2000. *The State of Food Insecurity in the World 2000*; J.R. Lupien and V. Menza. 1999. Assessing prospects for improving food security and nutrition. *Food, Nutrition and Agriculture*, No. 25.

erbated by a lack of education and capital, which are essential for freeing people from poverty.

Ineffective guardianship of the global commons

A second interrelated issue is the inadequate guardianship of the global commons, that is the resources, institutions and values that societies commonly share, yet which tend to be overexploited because of individual egoism. Three distinct aspects of guardianship are of concern here: natural resources, cultural identity and human rights.

Natural resources
Humanity's power to modify the natural world as well as our increasing numbers pose immense threats to the natural resource base on which we depend. Regarding marine resources, for instance, although the United Nations Convention on the Law

of the Sea (1982) was a step in the right direction, our collective ability to create ever-more effective means of catching fish is depleting the seas of much of their abundance and the majority of stocks are now fully exploited (Figure 4). Huge vessels with canneries on board compete with fishers using simple nets or lines. Entire communities based on fishing activities are suddenly discovering that their livelihoods are threatened.

Policies of increased industrial production threaten not merely to create local pollution but also to upset the climate, resulting in holes in the ozone layer as well as global warming. Current predictions suggest that, with global warming, we can expect more variable and harsher weather conditions, rising sea levels and inundated coastal cities, and shifts in the location of agricultural production.

Increases in the demand for water for agricultural, industrial and domestic uses are lowering groundwater levels and, in some cases, permanently depleting aquifers. In other cases, overuse of water is leading to the salinization and eventual abandonment of what was once prime agricultural land.

FIGURE 4
World capture fisheries reaches maximum potential

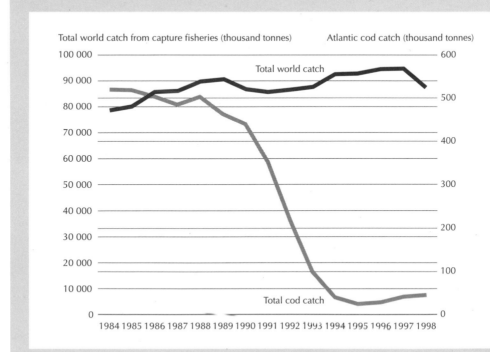

Source: FAO data, 2000.

Biodiversity, commonly considered essential for maintaining life on earth, is threatened as a result of widespread specialization in agricultural production (Figures 5 and 6), industrial pollution, deforestation and the introduction of invasive species.

FIGURE 5
Today's limited use of plant biodiversity for food production

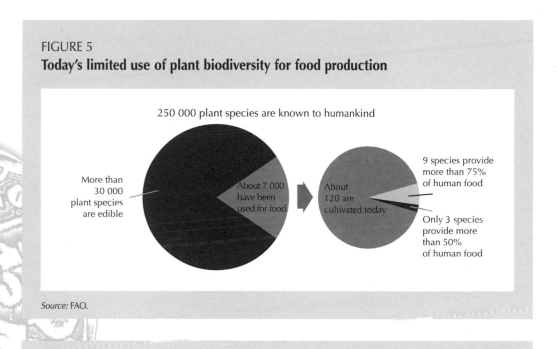

Source: FAO.

FIGURE 6
Proportion of the world's farm animal breeds at risk, by region

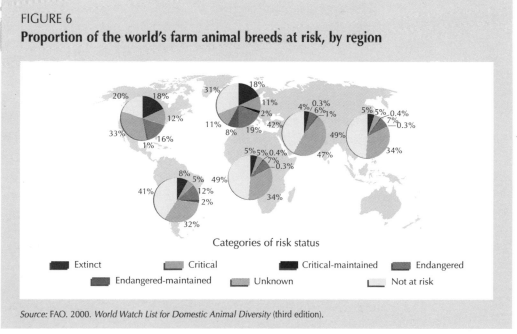

Source: FAO. 2000. *World Watch List for Domestic Animal Diversity* (third edition).

In short, entire ecosystems are being weakened, damaged and even destroyed by human intervention.

Cultural identity and diversity

The erosion of biodiversity is mirrored by the erosion of cultural diversity. Just as biodiversity may serve as insurance against unfavourable ecosystem changes, so cultural diversity may serve as a buffer against human error. Some cultures have proved exceedingly adept at incorporating new ideas and new technologies while reaffirming central values. Others have collapsed in the face of change. As markets penetrate previously isolated cultures, entire languages, traditions and practices, religions, types of food and means of food preparation and other social institutions are in danger of extinction. This is especially true of cultures whose primary values are non-material.

Some cultures have been eroded by national policies that foster conformity to the dominant national culture. Still others have been severely damaged by new technologies that undermine deeply held beliefs, thereby taking much of the meaning out of people's daily life. Some have been pushed aside for what is arguably defined as progress. The pervasiveness of advertising and the creation of truly international consumers of global foods, clothing, cinema and even music, have also increased the process of homogenization and obliterated cultural identities.

This is not to suggest that members of such cultures passively accept unwanted change. In fact, they often attempt to fight against the collapse of their cultural identity through increased cultural solidarity and resistance to externally induced change. Such resistance is often violent, resulting in loss of life and property as well as undermining democratic institutions and suppressing internal dissent. In the more extreme cases, resistance movements turn on themselves as partisans attempt to eliminate all those who do not live up to claimed traditional ideals.

Individuals' and peoples' rights

The simultaneous loss of biological and cultural diversity threatens to undermine the rights of both individuals and entire peoples. On the one hand, some groups would force people to abandon their age-old ways in order to partake of what is dubiously described as progress. On the other hand, there are those who would deprive indigenous populations of the conveniences of modern life, preserving them so that they can maintain global goods such as plant germplasm. Both extremes undermine the rights of individuals and peoples to make their own decisions and determine their future.

In all societies, traditional mechanisms to ensure the right to adequate food are being eroded by the weakening of social and cultural ties, brought about by the breakup of traditional family units, accelerated urbanization and the globalization of markets, information and culture. In the face of persistent and widespread hunger, therefore, the 1996 Rome Declaration on World Food Security and the World Food Summit Plan of Action reaffirmed the right of everyone to have access to safe and nutritious food and specified the need to clarify the definition of the right to food. They also reaffirmed the fundamental right of everyone to be free from hunger, as stated in the International Covenant on Economic, Social and Cultural Rights and other relevant international and regional instruments, urging particular attention to the implementation and full and progressive realization of these rights as a means of achieving food security for all.

An emerging global economy, but not a global society

While the globalization of the world's economy is proceeding rapidly, the creation of a global society is only now beginning to be considered. Goods, services and especially capital flow freely across national borders at ever-increasing rates, yet people remain largely constrained by national borders. For nations, businesses and consumers, action in the market is limited by access to capital; those without any means have no voice in the marketplace. And although every nation has institutions that supplement market forces with some form of social safety net to support people who are unable to draw adequate benefit from the market, the solidarity network among nations is rather underdeveloped.

Yet, a global market without a global society could be self-destructive. First, it may divide people between those who participate in the market and those who lack the means to do so, both within nations and among them. Whether it be for lack of education and capital or because they are exploited, those who cannot participate will reject the global market as yet another threat to their livelihoods. Second, the global market might involve the construction of international institutions that claim the allegiance of only a small élite. Citizens in both industrialized and developing nations may therefore reject global markets, plunging the world into conflicts at the national and international levels.

In contrast, little attention has been given to the prerequistes for building a global society. Such a society would embody the values put forth in dozens of international treaties and declarations that treat people as *citizens* rather than *consumers*. But how can we build a global society in which poverty, hunger and malnutrition are reduced or, better, eliminated?

Clearly, to achieve this goal, many diverse interests must be reconciled and several complex and protracted conflicts resolved. Other choices are conceivable but not attractive. There may be parties who believe they can triumph over others but, in the long term, there are no winners. No matter how difficult it may be, people must recognize that their fate is bound to that of others, as is the fate of the planet. A way must be found to reduce the gaps between the poor and the affluent, the food-secure and the food-insecure and the winners and losers of globalization as well as between cultures and between generations. •

Balancing interests and resolving conflicts

The gap between the poorest and the most affluent societies is growing

The gap between the poor and the affluent

Far too many people in the world remain marginalized. The gap between the poorest and the most affluent is growing. The poorest nations of the world have barely felt the impact of the global marketplace. Even many industrialized nations now have soaring unemployment levels and income inequalities not seen since the nineteenth century. The extremely small proportions of GDP devoted to foreign assistance attest to the "aid fatigue" found in most affluent nations. Furthermore, foreign assistance has not been as effective as it might have been. Charity – whether for individuals or for nations – responds to short-term needs, but it fails to create the necessary conditions for humans' self-respect and dignity.

Charity, or aid, responds only to short-term needs and fails to foster self-respect or dignity

Poor nations must be able to determine their own future, rather than having it defined for them by donors. Similarly, within nations, poor citizens must be the architects of their own destiny. True national security cannot be secured by military means; it can only be secured by providing all citizens the wherewithal to live their lives with dignity and justice. Nor is it possible to create a world that is equitable, just, legitimate and democratic solely via appeals to self-interest. Markets are human institutions. They *create* self-interested individuals who compete under highly restricted conditions and who may attempt to insulate themselves from the core goals of society at large. Even if markets are enthusiastically embraced, institutions must be designed in order to ensure freer and fairer competition. Among other things, efficient markets require organization, planning, well-defined property rights, rules of exchange and a clear and enforceable distinction between the public and private sectors.

Moreover, markets are just one means of distributing goods. There are certain things that all societies agree should not be bought and sold in the market, for example human beings, votes, justice and divine grace. These and other goods or services, such as the guarantee of survival, must be provided in different ways. All societies recognize the diverse *needs* of their citizenry (for instance the need of the poor and hungry to be given free food). Similarly, all societies recognize that some people *deserve* certain goods (such as medals or prizes) or "bads" (such as imprisonment in the case of murder). All societies have a notion of "public goods"; they are determined in terms of what members of a community or society commonly see as desirable. Individuals may be affected differently by the policies that societies adopt to ensure the adequate availability of public goods. Something that is considered a good in the sphere of health is not necessarily a good in the sphere of agricultural production. It is the contradictions among the different spheres that are a source of never-ending conflicts, negotiations and compromises in all societies. Thus, solutions to conflicts should be sought not by enforcing conformity to a single concept of justice, but by mediating among many different concepts. These conflicts may not be avoided, but institutions can be devised to contain and limit them.

The gap between the food-secure and the food-insecure

Although the right to food has repeatedly been reaffirmed as a fundamental human right (e.g. by the Rome Declaration on World Food Security, 1996), there is considerable disagreement as to how to realize this right in practice. Furthermore, while the strategy to ensure food security is laid out in the World Food Summit Plan of Action, the degree to which this Plan is being implemented varies significantly among countries.

Achieving food security requires: i) an *abundance* of food; ii) *access* to that food by everyone; iii) nutritional *adequacy*; and iv) *food safety*. At the world level, there is abundant food, yet there are distribution and access problems that result in about 800 million people not having enough food. For some, access to food can be assured by providing direct access to land. For the burgeoning urban populations, access depends on good farm-to-market roads, farm production that is well above subsistence levels, price structures that provide incentives to produce for the market, accurate market information for producers, food processing industries to transform raw products into storable foods and employment that permits people to earn enough to purchase food. In places where full employment is lacking, consumer subsidies (either through grants of food or through monetary grants to purchase food) are also essential to

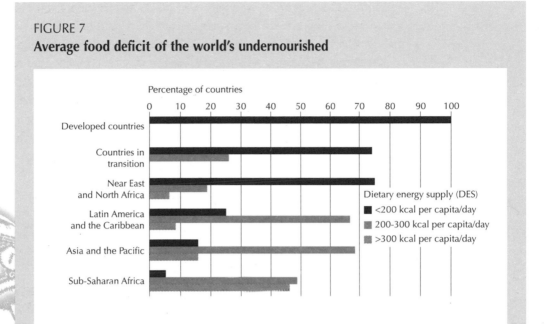

FIGURE 7
Average food deficit of the world's undernourished

Source: FAO. 2000. *The State of Food Insecurity in the World 2000.*

ensure access to food. To guarantee adequate food supplies for a growing population in the future, investment in research (an endless task, as the agricultural environment is continuously changing) as well as the conservation of agricultural land, forest and water resources are needed.

Food must also provide a nutritionally adequate diet. Today, some 12 million children die annually of nutrition-related diseases. Doubtless, far more are chronically ill. Nutritional needs must therefore be considered both in agricultural research and in food assistance programmes. Finally, food must be safe to eat. While this seems self-evident, the fact is that food-borne illness remains a frequent occurrence throughout the world. Microbial food contaminants are common, especially in urban areas, where food must travel long distances before consumption. The poorest are the most likely victims but, as world food trade expands, consumers in wealthy nations are also being affected by food-borne diseases.

The gap between the winners and losers of globalization

As noted above, the globalization of markets and technological developments have increased the interdependence among nations and cultures. Time and space have imploded; fences between nations have been lowered. But interdependence does not imply equity, equality of opportunity, justice or even compassion. There is no automatic process by which markets can ensure the realization of these widely held values. Nor can markets be the universal solution, reconciling all values by economic means. Indeed, markets do not concern people's shared values or collective rights and duties as citizens; rather they concern their roles as producers and consumers. In other words, people's ethical obligations must be worked out through political processes and not be reduced to market administration.

Thus, the global challenge is to develop institutional means to ensure that losses suffered as a result of market forces do not violate basic rights, bring widespread hunger or cause the immiserization of individuals, families, communities or states. Although there have been proposals to redress the grievances of losers, these have rarely, if ever, been brought to fruition. An alternative approach could be the expansion of civil society beyond the nation state, in which case all citizens would feel responsible for all people as well as for the earth as a whole and they would participate in the democratic control of the market.

At the same time, members of a global civil society would engage in the construction of a better world, by inventing better means for peaceful conflict resolution, ensuring global financial stability, managing the global environment, managing global markets, establishing global standards and promoting sustainable development. The realization of such goals, however, is often blocked by a lack of jurisdiction, participation and incentives. Even if these obstacles can be overcome, the goals must be achieved without creating bloated bureaucracies; indeed, these would destroy the very processes they were designed to foster. Nor should progress in attaining global goals require discarding national sovereignty.

The global economy will acquire its long-term justification only if it is a means to further fundamental human values. States cannot be accountable solely to foreign investors, fund managers and domestic exporters. Fundamental values cannot be actualized by an élite or by decree: because they are sometimes contradictory, values require democratic deliberation, dialogue and discourse. Thus, all states need to develop new means of democratic participation in the fundamental decisions that affect people's lives.

Globalization underscores the importance of the diversity of "place". To say that a process is global is not to say that it happens in exactly the same way everywhere. Rather, it means that it "acts at a distance". Thus, FAO is global only to the extent that it can act at a distance; that is, a decision made in Rome – a distinct, local place – can affect people 10 000 kilometres away. Place continues to be local in character, with a local culture, ecology and economy. Thus, both losers and winners are always geographically and socially placed; it is never a matter of those who are global and cosmopolitan versus those who are local and parochial. Rather, it is a matter of those who, for a variety of reasons, can act at a distance and those who cannot.

When conflicts emerge over access to natural resources, they are not caused by disputes between global and local forces. They result from disputes between those able to act at a distance and those unable to do so. Often, such external interests are able to encroach on weaker communities, leading to impoverishment and marginalization. Although Principle 2 of the Rio Declaration on Environment and Development (1992) reasserts the sovereignty of states, states have not always been good stewards of such resources. All too often they have been used by an élite in collusion with external actors to crush community opposition. Action is needed to strengthen the capacity of weaker communities to defend their rights in the face of encroachment by their own state or by other foreign actors. This will require institutionalizing mechanisms of self-restraint for both states and transnational companies to ensure that the rights of weaker groups are recognized and respected. At the same time, it will require giving a greater voice to weaker communities through participatory management of natural resources.

Global development policies make little sense if they are not viewed through the lens of national and local development policies. Rather than a well-presented, grand plan for development that meets the demand for rationality on paper but fails in the field, what is needed are social mechanisms allowing the development of far messier plans that achieve their rationality by employing the wealth of intelligence and creativity emerging from democratic participation. Participatory management cannot be an afterthought, tacked on after a policy or project has been designed and is ready to be implemented. It must be a central element from the very inception of a project. One way to pursue this goal is through "collaborative management", whereby the relevant stakeholders are substantially involved in management activities. Such a system would be flexible and adaptable to differences in places and times. It would involve a partnership among affected communities, nations and the private sector, civil society and international organizations.

The gap between cultures

The World Commission on Culture and Development (1995) has noted that culture is often ignored in development theory and practice. Yet, economic development does not take place in a vacuum. It transforms and is transformed by cultures, often for the better, but sometimes to the detriment of one or the other. As noted above, globalization simultaneously homogenizes and fragments cultures. The challenge is to distinguish between the tasks that must be accomplished as part of humanity's commonality and the plurality of views and practices that are essential for the full development of human capacities, both individual and collective.

We need not all follow identical paths to development. We need not arrange our values in the same way everywhere and for all times. We need not treat cultural diversity as an obstacle to be overcome. Homogeneity does not ensure social solidarity any more than heterogeneity guarantees conflict. Just as we need a division of labour in order to create a complex society, so we need multiple perspectives and practices to build a global society. The challenge is to ensure respect for differences without fragmentation and isolation, to promote consensus on values and practices without imposing a stifling uniformity on everyone. To meet this challenge, respect for pluralism must be enhanced among nations as well as within nations and at the level of institutions, and dialogue and debate need to be pursued within cultures to allow for their evolution.

The gap between generations

The preamble to the Stockholm Declaration on the Human Environment (1972) acknowledged the signatories' realization that "to defend and improve the human environment for present and future generations had become an imperative goal for mankind". The World Charter for Nature (1982) and the Rio Declaration on Environment and Development (1992) reaffirm that commitment. This is not a commitment to specific individuals who do not as yet exist. Instead, it is an obligation not to do anything that would impose unending and onerous duties on future generations. In other words, we need to: i) conserve options that those who succeed us might wish to pursue; ii) ensure that the planet is not left in a worse condition than when we inherited it; and iii) conserve the legacy of the past so that future generations might have access to it.

We must conserve options that those who succeed us might wish to pursue

One means by which the rights of future generations might be safeguarded is through use of the precautionary principle as set forth in numerous documents, including the Rio Declaration on Environment and Development (1992), the Earth Charter (2000), the Convention on Biological Diversity (1992) and the Cartagena Protocol on Biosafety (2000). The precautionary principle, simply put, asserts that in areas where scientific knowledge is lacking and/or where levels of uncertainty with respect to deleterious effects are high, one should proceed with extreme caution:

> "... Where there are threats of serious or irreversible damage, lack of full scientific certainty shall not be used as a reason for postponing cost-effective measures to prevent environmental degradation."
>
> **Rio Declaration on Environment and Development, Principle 15**

This applies particularly to those instances where decisions are irreversible. Our duty to future generations can also be examined through the lens of sustainability. However, sustainability has many definitions. Environmentalists often define it as "avoidance of use", while some involved in agriculture define it as "production without reducing soil fertility". Sustainability is often so broadly or narrowly interpreted that it provides little guidance for action. Indeed, some highly exploitive systems might be sustainable for centuries. A more balanced approach might define agricultural sustainability as a form of stewardship that attempts to respect nature, conserve resources, engage in agriculture and achieve equity and justice. Such an approach would also recognize that no agricultural practices are without potential for irony and tragedy; no human plans are perfect.

No matter what the approach may be, there is little doubt that we are in the process of rethinking and renegotiating our relations with the natural world. Our duty to future generations is inextricably bound to the care with which we treat nature. •

Building a more equitable and ethical food and agriculture system

FAO has constitutional obligations to raise levels of nutrition and standards of living, to secure improvements in the efficiency of the production and distribution of all food and agricultural products, to better the conditions of rural populations, and thus to contribute to an expanding world economy and to ensuring humanity's freedom from hunger. In addition, FAO is mandated by the international community to provide the instruments and mechanisms for an international forum in which to address and take action on the balancing of interests while aiming to protect and enhance global public goods that are relevant for food and agriculture (FAO Constitution, 1945; Rome Declaration on World Food Security, 1996). Moreover, FAO has an ethical obligation to ensure that its actions are responsible, transparent and accountable as well as to provide a forum for debate and dialogue on ethical issues and unethical behaviour with respect to food and agriculture.

These instruments and mechanisms can be employed to build a more equitable, ethically-based food and agriculture system that addresses the issues and challenges described above. It would be efficient, safe and solidary, while respecting the diversity of value systems. Building such a system does not and should not mean merely creating a blueprint – a detailed plan that risks becoming an end in itself. Instead, it must be a participatory process as well as one that evolves over time in response to new scientific data, changes in goals and objectives and new ethical issues raised by FAO and its partners.

A more equitable, ethically-based, food and agriculture system must incorporate concern for three widely accepted global goals, each of which incorporate numerous normative propositions: improved well-being, protection of the environment and improved public health.

Improved well-being

Poverty remains the single most important cause of human misery in the world today. Participants in an equitable, ethically-based food and agriculture system would work towards the reduction and eventual elimination of poverty by enhancing economic efficiency and effectiveness in food and agriculture worldwide. In so doing, production efficiency (the most efficient means of producing a given good) must be balanced with distribution efficiency (the most efficient means of distributing goods). Moreover, efficiency cannot be judged solely in terms of relative cost within a particular economic system. It must also include study of the system of rights, privileges and institutions according to which efficiency is defined. Similarly, effectiveness cannot be defined merely as the ability to accomplish a particular task; it must also be measured in terms of the appropriateness of the means selected in light of ethical concerns such as fairness and justice.

In addition, efficiency and effectiveness cannot be promoted at the expense of economic interdependence, individual freedom, human rights or state sovereignty. Instead, efficiency must contribute to these goals. In other words, an ethical food and agriculture system must help citizens, communities, nations and the world as a whole progress from a global economy towards a truly global society.

In such a society, interdependence would be recognized as inescapable, each individual would be granted personal autonomy and dignity, and states would be able to maintain their sovereignty. An ethical food and agriculture system must also move from free trade, in which powerful interests are able to impose their rules in the marketplace, to an ethics-based trading system that comprises a participatory mode for establising and implementing rules.

Protection of the environment

Viewed from a global perspective, food is not currently produced in the places or ways that best conserve natural resources. In the past, global agricultural production tended to mirror the dietary patterns and living standards of local populations. This pattern is rapidly changing worldwide, with increasing urbanization, market penetration and international trade. In order to maintain an equitable, ethically-based food and agriculture system, biological efficiency (through enhanced production, processing and distribution of food and agricultural products) and agrobiological diversity must be reconciled with economic efficiency. This would allow food to be produced with a minimum use of resources, thus limiting the pressure on the environment and making food affordable for the poor. Careful consideration needs to be given to the management of the trade-offs between the objectives of food security and environmental protection. Integrated pest management and integrated resource management in agriculture, forestry and fisheries should not be considered luxuries; if an equitable, ethically-based food and agriculture system is to be passed on to future generations, they are necessities.

Improved public health

Despite some improvements over the last several decades, far too large a portion of the world's population suffers from poor health brought on by hunger, malnutrition, poor diet and unsafe food and water. These problems diminish the ability of people to participate fully in the daily affairs of their community or nation or of the world. Moreover, large-scale industrialization of agriculture and food processing poses new health threats when it is not properly monitored and controlled.

In an equitable, ethically-based food and agriculture system, issues of hunger, malnutrition, diet and food safety would be aggressively addressed, so the world would rapidly reach a stage where everyone had access to an abundant, nutritionally adequate and safe diet. Achieving this will require: i) policies that provide incentives for distributional changes to reduce inequalities in access to food; ii) scientific research to develop more efficient, safer means of food production, processing and distribution; iii) rural development to promote and develop sources of clean drinking-water and to encourage the use of safe food handling practices; and iv) the use and enforcement of adequate safeguards and safety standards in the deployment of new products.

First step

No single set of ethical principles is sufficient for building a more equitable and ethical food and agriculture system, given that it is the conflicts and contradictions among these very principles that are at issue. But individuals, states, corporations and voluntary organizations in the international community can help progress to be made through the following actions:

Creating the mechanisms necessary to balance interests and resolve conflicts. This can be accomplished by establishing fora in which controversies can be discussed and carried towards a resolution. For example, the Commission on Genetic Resources for Food and Agriculture has been successful in providing a forum for discussing difficult issues, including compatibilities and complementarities between plant breeders' and farmers' rights. Further examples are the agreements achieved on food standards by the Codex Alimentarius Commission or principles contained in the Code of Conduct for Responsible Fisheries (1995).

Supporting and encouraging broad stakeholder participation in policies, programmes and projects. Diverse standpoints should be represented on all international bodies. New means for participation by non-governmental organizations as well as by interested and informed citizens should be invented.

Encouraging individuals, communities and nations to engage in dialogue and, ultimately, to do what is ethical. Incentives that will encourage behaviour that promotes the values presented above (e.g. fair trade) are desirable, while incentives to engage in unethical behaviour must be removed. This process will be an iterative one, learning from past experiences with particular incentives and modifying future incentives so as to avoid unintended consequences.

Developing and disseminating widely the information and analyses necessary to make wise and ethical decisions. Information must be timely, relevant, accurate and easily accessible to all stakeholders. It must reach diverse audiences through various media, including print, television, radio and Web-based publications.

Ensuring that decision-making procedures in international food and agriculture policy as well as the content of deliberations are well understood and open to public scrutiny. No matter how democratic and fair decisions are, without public scrutiny or awareness of them, their fairness and appropriateness cannot be judged. In contrast, public scrutiny and public understanding of decision-making processes as well as the content of actual decisions will contribute to the development of a more ethical, robust and effective global food and agriculture system.

Fostering the use of science and technology in support of a more just and equitable food and agriculture system. This will require the reconciliation of expert knowledge with indigenous knowledge and with diverse, deeply held cultural beliefs concerning priorities and values as well as appropriate action. In particular, it must be recognized that while science may inform us about levels of risk in a given undertaking, it cannot tell us whether a risk is worth taking. This question can only be addressed through dialogue among parties likely to be affected.

Ensuring that programmes, policies, standards and decisions always take ethical considerations into account so as to lead to enhanced well-being, environmental protection and improved health. Included here is an obligation to draw attention to situations and trends that decrease well-being, degrade the environment or constitute barriers to health. At the same time, it must be recognized that these three goals are not always congruent. Consequently, even if all parties agree on the ethical goals, an ongoing dialogue must take place to reconcile those goals in particular settings. That dialogue must necessarily involve negotiations and compromises as well as different means of resolution in different places.

Developing codes of ethical conduct where they do not currently exist. In a diverse and interdependent world, considerations for ethical conduct must be clear to all. Just as is now common in various professions, those individuals, states, corporations and voluntary organizations involved in building an equitable global food and agriculture system need guidance as to what constitutes ethical behaviour. Codes of conduct can provide that guidance.

Periodically reviewing ethical commitments and determining whether or not they are appropriate, in the light of new knowledge and changes in circumstances. The world today is changing rapidly. What is taken to be true today may be found to be false tomorrow. What is considered ethical today may be considered unethical tomorrow. Thus, no definitive blueprint for ethical behaviour and action is possible. What is necessary is that ethical positions be reviewed regularly to see how they might be improved on the basis of new evidence, new requirements and new demands. •

References

INTERNATIONAL INSTRUMENTS AND BODIES CITED

Code of Conduct for Responsible Fisheries (1995)

Codex Alimentarius Commission (1963)

Commission on Genetic Resources for Food and Agriculture (1995),
formerly the Commission on Plant Genetic Resources (1983)

Convention on Biological Diversity (1992) and Cartagena Protocol
on Biosafety (2000)

Earth Charter (2000)

FAO Constitution (1945)

Rio Declaration on Environment and Development (1992)

Rome Declaration on World Food Security (1996)

Stockholm Declaration on the Human Environment (1972)

United Nations Convention on the Law of the Sea (1982)

United Nations Framework Convention on Climate Change (1992)

Universal Declaration of Human Rights (1948)

WHO Constitution (1946)

World Charter for Nature (1982)

World Commission on Culture and Development (1995)

SUGGESTED FURTHER READING

Bock, C. & Sharif, A. 1997. Conflicts over natural resources. *Development*, 40: 85-90.

FAO. 1998. *The state of the world's plant genetic resources for food and agriculture.* Rome, FAO.

Hulse, J.H. 1995. *Science, agriculture, and food security.* Ottawa, National Research Council of Canada.

Jamieson, D. 1998. Sustainability and beyond. *Ecological Economics*, 24: 183-192.

Kaul, I., Grunberg, I. & Stern, M.A., eds. 1999. *Global public goods: international cooperation in the 21st century.* Oxford, UK, University of Oxford Press.

Morin, E. & Kern, A.B. 1999. *Homeland earth: a manifesto for the new millennium.* Cresskill, New Jersey, USA, Hampton Press.

Rodrik, D. 1999. *The new global economy and developing countries: making openness work.* Baltimore, USA, Johns Hopkins University Press.

Serres, M. 1995. *The natural contract.* Ann Arbor, USA, University of Michigan Press.

Thompson, P. 1995. *The spirit of the soil: agriculture and environmental ethics.* London, Routledge.

UNDP. 1999. *Human Development Report 1999.* Oxford, UK, University of Oxford Press.

Weiss, E.B. 1989. *In fairness to future generations: international law, common patrimony, and intergenerational equity.* Tokyo, UNU.

In a diverse and interdependent world, considerations for ethical conduct must be clear to all